Action Sports Library

Sailboarding

Bob Italia

Published by Abdo & Daughters, 6535 Cecilia Circle, Edina, Minnesota 55439.

Library bound edition distributed by Rockbottom Books, Pentagon Tower, P.O. Box 36036, Minneapolis, Minnesota 55435.

Printed in the United States.

ISBN: 1-56239-078-3

Library of Congress Card Catalog Number: 91-073019

Cover Photos: ©ALLSPORT USA/PHOTOGRAPHER, 1991.
Inside Photos: ©ALLSPORT USA/PHOTOGRAPHER, 1991.

Warning: The series *Action Sports Library* is intended as entertainment for children. These sporting activities should never be attempted without the proper conditioning, training, instruction, supervision, and equipment.

Edited by Rosemary Wallner

CONTENTS

Sailboarding—combining surfing and sailing
for the ultimate water sport!

SAILBOARDING

How it all Began

Sailboarding (also known as windsurfing) was developed in California in 1967 by Hoyle Schweitzer and Jim Drake. They wanted to develop a new sport that would allow them to enjoy sailing without having to spend a lot of time preparing the rigging. They were also tired of the surfing crowds and didn't want to rely on good wave conditions to perform their activity.

The first sailboard, called a "Baja Board," was a simple design. It had a sail and a mast that could swivel in all directions.

By 1969, Schweitzer started a company that manufactured these boards. He called the company Windsurfer® and began traveling the country promoting and selling these new water sport devices.

But Schweitzer did not have a lot of money and could not produce many boards. So in 1970, Ten Cate, a Dutch textile manufacturer offered to help manufacture the boards and the sails. By 1971, sailboarding was a major sport in Europe.

Sailboarding did not catch on in the United States until the early 1980s. In 1984, the International Olympic Committee adopted sailboarding as the seventh Olympic sailing event. Today over 100 companies around the world manufacture sailboards. Over 2 million have been sold. Sailboards can be found on every ocean on earth.

Types of Boards

There are five basic types of sailboards:

1) The Flatboard—this is the most popular sailboard. It is best for beginners and all-around use. It is flat and very stable.

2) The Pan Am Strong Wind Board—this board performs best in strong wind and is designed for racing. It is similar in shape to the flatboard, but it has footstraps.

3) The Open Class Roundboard—this is the best racing board available. It is longer and narrower than the flatboard and is more difficult to handle.

4) The Strong Wind Funboard—this board is designed for wave jumping and strong winds. It is very short and has footstraps.

5) The Sinker—This is the shortest board available, recommended for the expert only. It is ideal for rough surf and high winds, and has footstraps.

Clothing

Though special clothing is not needed to sailboard, it can make the sport more enjoyable. It's easy to sailboard in a swimsuit when it's sunny and warm—but what happens when the weather turns a little foul? Having a good sailboard suit, gloves and shoes can help a sailboarder enjoy the sport even when the air and water temperature are on the cool side.

Wetsuits are the most common sailboard clothing. A wetsuit is a skintight suit made of neoprene (man-made rubber). It traps a thin layer of water between the suit and your skin. The wearer's body temperature heats the thin layer of water and acts as an insulator, keeping the wearer warm in cool weather. A wetsuit should fit tight but still be comfortable. It should not restrict movement. If a wetsuit is too tight, it could cause muscle cramps.

Drysuits are another alternative. They are usually made of nylon. They keep your body dry. But drysuits are bulky and not as comfortable as wetsuits.

Sailboarding gloves are helpful in cool-weather sailing. They are made of neoprene and leather, with reinforced palms. Insulated sailboarding boots, also made of neoprene, can give a sailboarder added gripping power even if a board has a nonslip surface. There are also sailboarding shoes which are designed for extra grip and are not insulated.

Beginning

Sailboarding may look easy, but it's not. There are many techniques you must know before you can master the sport. The best way to learn how to sailboard is to enroll in a sailboarding course. They last only one or two days, and the instructors can teach you all the basics you'll need.

Before you start, you'll need to know the basic parts of the sailboard and its rigging. The board consists of the bow (nose), the stern (tail), the skeg (fin), the daggerboard (main fin), and the footstraps.

The sail rigging consists of the mast, which holds the sail, the boom (which you hold onto to steer the sail), and the sail itself.

Carrying the Rig

Getting the sail rigging down to the shore can be difficult especially if its windy. The best way is to grip the boom and the mast and carry the rigging over your head. Make sure you keep the boom pointing in the direction of the wind. This way, the sail won't act like a kite and blow away.

Rigging Up

One of the most important steps of sailboarding is rigging up. Without proper assembly of the sailboard, you run the risk of of equipment failure on the water.

Find an open space along the shore. Remove the sail from its bag and slide the mast into the mast sleeve of the sail. Then secure the mast into the mast foot of the board. Next adjust the

The proper way to carry a sailboard.

boom to shoulder height. Recheck all connections to make sure everything is secure.

Launching

If you're not careful during the launching of your sailboard, you may break some of the equipment. Launch the board and rigging together—not separately. Carry the front of the board under one arm and hold onto the front of the boom with the other. Then carefully drag the sailboard into the water.

Landing

When approaching the shore, raise the daggerboard and jump off the board while holding onto the mast. Then lift the tail of the board and push it onto the beach while maintaining your grip on the mast. Once you're out of the water, pivot the board around so that the front of the board is facing the water. Then slowly drag the board onto the shore.

Uphauling the Sail Rigging

Before you go out into the water, practice pulling the sail up (uphauling). Determine the direction of the wind, then place the board at a right angle to the wind. The sail rigging should be on the leeward side (the side opposite the windward side) of the board. In other words, your back should be to the wind and the rigging should be laying in front of you.

Step onto the board, placing one foot on either side of the mast. Grab the rope that is attached to the mast and assume a squatting position. Now gradually pull the mast up with the rope and straighten your legs. Do it slowly. The sail is full of water and will be very heavy.

Once the sail is out of the water, keep pulling up the mast with the rope. Don't worry about the flapping sail. The wind will keep it away from you. Once the mast is upright, you should be, too. Grab onto the front of the boom. You are now ready to sail!

Uphauling the Sail Rigging from the Windward Side

Occasionally you may find that you must pull the sail up from the windward side (with the wind in your face). This is a more difficult maneuver, but one you should also practice before you go out into the water.

Position the board at a right angle to the wind and place the rigging to the windward side. Stand on the board as before and grab the rope attached to the mast. Now carefully pull the mast up with the rope.

Once the sail is clear of the water, the wind will swing it around quickly. Let it go. As the sail crosses over the board, move your feet around the mast to balance the board. You should be facing the same direction as the board. When the sail is on the leeward side, continue to move your feet around the mast until your back is facing the wind. Now you are in the same position as when you were practicing uphauling on the leeward side. Slowly straighten your legs as you pull the sail up, then grab onto the boom. You might need to practice this very difficult maneuver several times.

Sailing

Once you've uphauled the sail rigging and have a firm grip of the boom, pull the sail towards you. The sail will begin to fill with wind and the board will start to move. Make sure you lean backward. The stronger the wind, the more you will have to lean back. Otherwise, the wind will pull you over. The closer you pull the sail to you, the faster you will go.

Rotating the Board

Sometimes when you are uphauling the rigging, you will find that the board has turned in the wrong direction. (Remember, you always want the board to be pointing at a right angle to the wind.)

To turn the board, hold the sail by the boom and rotate the board with your feet until it is pointing the way you want it. Then grab the boom and pull the sail towards you.

A Good Sailing Stance

To get the most out of sailboarding, a good sailing stance is important. Your back should always be straight and your knees slightly bent. When the wind increases, lean back to counter the force. If the wind gets too strong, let go of the boom and hold onto the mast or the mast rope.

Keeping the board flat is also important. Try to keep your balance near the center of the board—not too far forward, leeward or windward. Try to relax and enjoy the ride. The more you practice, the easier it will become.

Stopping

Learning to stop is just as important as learning how to start. Knowing how to stop can prevent damage to your board and personal injury.

To stop, remove one hand from the boom and grip the mast below the boom. Then remove the other hand from the boom, crouch, and grab the mast. Both hands should be on the mast.

Allow the rigging to fall away from you as you continue to squat. Once the sail reaches the water, the board will stop.

Advanced Sailboarding Maneuvers

Once you've mastered the basic sailboard techniques, you'll want to practice some advanced maneuvers.

• Tacking—If you want to sail to a point that's upwind (into the wind), you'll need to zigzag your way there. This is called tacking. Start by pointing the board into the wind. Tilt the sail rigging back and carefully position yourself in front of the mast. Now move to the other side of the sail as the board begins to turn. Grab the boom and pull the sail towards you. Now you have turned slightly and are sailing a new course upwind. After you sailed this new course for a while, repeat the process to set a new course. After tacking back and forth upwind, you will eventually reach your destination.

- Gybing—This is the opposite of tacking, when you want to zigzag downwind (with the wind behind you). Start by gripping the boom with both hands. Point the board downwind and stand behind the mast. Now let go of the boom with your back hand and grip the front of the boom. Allow the sail to swing in front of you. This will make the board turn slightly. Grip the middle of the boom and pull the sail towards you. Now the sail is on the other side of the board. Repeat the process until you zigzag your way downwind to your destination.

- Water Starts—Water starts used to be considered a freestyle trick. Now they are considered a normal maneuver. Once you've mastered them, water starts are much easier and less tiring than standing on the board and uphauling the sail rigging.

Begin by getting the mast at a right angle to the wind. (Remember, you're in the water, so you'll have to swing the mast into the proper position). Now hold the mast with your front hand. Start treading water and push the mast up so that the boom is out of the water. When the wind begins to lift the sail, grab onto the boom and swim closer to the board. Place your back foot on the tail of the board and tread the water with your front foot. This will give you added lift. Now place your weight on your back foot and, keeping your leg bent, lift yourself onto the board. Hold your arms high to keep the rigging up. Once the board begins to move, raise your front foot onto the board. You're up—and you're sailing!

Wind Speeds

Taking note of wind speeds is important, especially if you're just a beginner. The Beaufort scale was created to help boaters and surfers gauge the wind. Use the scale to determine if the water is safe enough for you to venture out:

- Force 0...calm...no waves
- Force 1...light air...ripples
- Force 2...light breeze...small wavelets
- Force 3...gentle breeze...large wavelets
- Force 4...moderate breeze...small waves
- Force 5...fresh breeze...moderate waves
- Force 6...strong breeze...large waves with white crests
- Force 7...near gale...large breaking waves with foamy crests
- Force 8...gale...high waves
- Force 9...strong gale...high waves that topple over
- Force 10...storm...towering waves with long overhanging crests

- Force 11...violent storm...spray hides huge waves
- Force 12...hurricane...air filled with foam and spray

Beginners should not go out onto the water in winds that are over Force 3. If you suddenly find yourself out too far, don't leave your board. Dismantle the sail, roll it up around the mast, and lay it on the board. Then lay on top of the board and paddle back with your arms. If you cannot paddle, raise your arms above your head and wave them from side to side. This is the international distress signal and will alert others that you are in trouble.

Wave Sailing

Wave sailing is the most spectacular part of sailboarding. Wave sailing is done in oceans where the surf can get very active. To be a good wave sailor, you must have command

Wave sailing is a spectacular form
of sailboarding.

of the basic sailboarding skills. It also helps to have a short board, such as a sinker. The best wave sailors are also very good surfers. Many surfing techniques—too many to mention—make up good wave sailing techniques. If you want to become a wave sailor, lessons are recommended.

Wave Jumping

Wave jumping is the most difficult of all the sailboarding techniques. But it's also the most exciting. This is how it's done:

Attack the wave head-on. Shift your weight to your back foot. When the board meets the wave, shift your weight further back and lean toward the tail of the board. When the nose of the board clears the wave, pull up with your front foot and pull the sail towards you. Once the tail of the board leaves the wave, relax your front foot and kick your back foot towards the wind. This will allow

Wave jumping on a sailboard.

you to bank off the wind. To land, keep your weight on your back foot so that the tail of the board meets the water first. Cushion the landing by bending your knees.

If you lose control during a jump, you'll have to "bail out." Let go of the boom, kick your feet out of the footstraps, then push the board and the sail rigging away from you.

Upside-Down Jumps

As impossible as it may seem, you can learn to make upside-down jumps. Attack the wave head-on. When the nose of the board rises up the wave, lean your body back. When the middle of the board lifts from the wave, pull hard with your front foot and lean further back. Once the tail leaves the wave, kick it up over your head and into the wind. You are now upside-down!

When you begin to drop, bring the tail of the board under your body. Then land the board on the water tail first. Cushion your landing by bending your knees. An upside-down jump is a difficult but spectacular sailboarding maneuver.

Sailboard Competitions

The two most recognized sailboard racing events are the World Funboard Cup and the Euro Funboard Cup. These events are divided into three competitions: (1) course racing, (2) slalom racing, and (3) wave riding. Points are given for each contest, and the sailboarder with the most points at the end is declared the overall champion.

The sailboard racing events are held all over the world. Some of the most popular locations are the Hawaiian Islands, Lake Garda in Italy, the Mediterranean coast of France, the Canary Islands, and the west coast of Australia.

Competitive sailboarding events
are held all over the world.

A Final Word

No water sport has come so far so fast as sailboarding. In less than 15 years, sailboarding has developed from a strange version of surfing into an internationally recognized sport. As with all water sports, sailboarding takes a lot of practice to master. But once you have the skills, no other water sport can provide you with as much excitement.

GLOSSARY

- Boom—the long handle you hold onto to steer the sail.

- Bow—the front of a sailboard.

- Daggerboard—the main fin of the sailboard.

- Downwind—with the wind at your back.

- Drysuit—a nylon suit that keeps you dry while sailboarding.

- Footstraps—straps on the sailboard that secure your feet.

- Freestyle—a style of sailboarding that uses stunts.

- Gale—a very strong wind.

- Gybing—A sailboard maneuver that allows you to zigzag downwind.

- Leeward side—the side of the sailboard opposite the wind.

- Mast—the upright pole that holds the sail.

- Neoprene—a man-made rubber.

- Rigging—the mechanisms of the sail.

- Rigging up—to put together the sailboard.

- Slalom racing—a sailboard race that zigzags through a course marked with buoys and flags.

- Skeg—the back fin of a sailboard.

- Stern—the back of the sailboard.

- Tacking—sailboarding to a point that's upwind.

- Uphauling—lifting the sail from the water.

- Upwind—into the wind.

- Water starts—a maneuver that allows you to begin sailboarding while lying in the water.

- Wavelets—very small waves.

- Wetsuit—skintight sailboard clothing made of neoprene that traps a thin layer of water between the suit and your skin.

- Windward side—the side of the sailboard that faces the wind.